The Somersetshire Co

A Pictorial Journey

Roger Halse & Simon Castens

Millstream Books

Somersetshire Coal Canal Company Boundary Stone
(Terry Paget collection)

cover illustrations:
(front) Upper Midford, c.1900. *(Tim Samler collection)*
(rear) Map of 5 Miles Round Bath, c.1850. *(Roger Halse collection)*

title page illustration: The barge 'Faith' at Chippenham Wharf, Wilts & Berks Canal, c.1900
Coal barges owned by W.H.Brinkworth, Coal Merchant, made regular trips from Chippenham to
Camerton. At its peak, the Wilts & Berks Canal carried nearly 56,000 tons of north Somerset coal
annually, with the branch to Chippenham carrying over 9,500 tons. *(Gerald Quartley collection)*

First published in June 2000 by Millstream Books, 18 The Tyning, Widcombe, Bath BA2 6AL

Set in Palatino and printed in Great Britain by The Jensen Press, Yeovil, Somerset

© Roger Halse & Simon Castens 2000

ISBN 094897558X

British Library Cataloguing-in-Publication Data: a catalogue record for this book is available from the British Library

Acknowledgements

For permission to use photographs, special thanks to Len Bampfylde, Trustees of the Bath Royal Literary & Scientific Institution, Bill Boyling, John Broome, Max & Angela Crofts, Paul De'Ath, Alan Dodge, Mrs. L. Ellis, Bob Hallam, Monkton Combe School, Natural History Museum, Sandy Neill, John New, Terry Paget, Neil Parkhouse, Julian Peters, Gerald Quartley, Philip Raby, Tim & Anne Samler, Freda Shellard, Museum of the Great Western Railway, Mike Tozer, Tony Wadley, Tim & Wendy Wheeldon; for help in processing the photographic print of the SCC wharf in Widcombe, Michael Gray; for their help in drawing the maps, Mike Chapman and Carole Haines. We are especially grateful to Tim Graham of Millstream Books without whose help this book would not have been possible. Finally, our thanks are due to the Somersetshire Coal Canal Society, founded in 1992, whose interest and efforts in furthering research into the history of the canal and in restoring and preserving its structures and line have helped not only to ensure the survival of what remains of the canal, but have provided the impetus for the gathering of this photographic collection. Details of the Society can be obtained from Laurie Gibney, 1 Hillcrest Close, Nailsea, Bristol BS48 2HP (tel: 01275 798479; e-mail: laurie@lgibney.freeserve co.uk). Information can also be found on the following web site – http://homepages.enterprise.net/rtj/SCC2.html.

Bibliography

Allsop, Niall, *The Somersetshire Coal Canal Rediscovered*, Millstream Books, 1988
Allsop, Niall, *Images of the Kennet & Avon*, Redcliffe Press, 1987
Batten, Chisholm E., *The Centenary of William Smith*, Proceedings of the Somerset Archaeology & Natural History Society, 1892
Clew, Kenneth R., *The Somersetshire Coal Canal and Railways*, David & Charles, 1970
Clew, Kenneth R., *The Kennet & Avon Canal*, David & Charles, 1968
Dalby, L. J., *The Wilts & Berks Canal*, Oakwood Press, 1971
Down, C. G. & Warrington, A. J., *The History of the Somerset Coalfield*, David & Charles, 1971
Gilson, R. G. & Quartley, G.W., *Some Technical Aspects of the Somerset Coal Canal Tramways*, Industrial Archaeology, Volume 5, 1968
Handley, Chris, *The Railways and Tramways of Radstock*, Somerset & Dorset Railway Trust, 1979
Handley, Chris, *Radstock Coal & Steam*, Volume 1, Millstream Books, 1991
Handley, Chris, *Radstock Coal & Steam*, Volume 2, Millstream Books, 1992
Maggs, Colin G. & Beale, Gerry, *The Camerton Branch*, Wild Swan, 1985
Priestley, Joseph, *A Historical Account of the Navigable Rivers, Canal, and Railways of Great Britain*, 1831; reprint, David & Charles, 1969
Warner, Richard, *Excursions from Bath*, 1800.

A Somersetshire Coal Canal Mile Post
Sited at every half-mile point along the northern line of the canal, these cast-iron plates, fixed to stone posts, indicated the distance from the junction of the Somersetshire Coal Canal with the Kennet & Avon Canal at Dundas.
(*Terry Paget collection*)

Preface

At the height of the industrial revolution the rural county of Somerset was a hive of activity; in particular, the area around Radstock, Paulton and Timsbury was busy with the mining of that important commodity to the growth of this revolution – coal. The necessity of finding cheaper and quicker means of transporting coal led to the rapid growth of the inland waterway network of navigable rivers and canals throughout England and Wales. The Somersetshire Coal Canal was an artery to this network and provided an important link in the transportation of fuel to the coal-hungry towns and rural villages of Somerset, Wiltshire and beyond.

This collection of photographs seeks not to provide a detailed history, but to give a glimpse of a once long-forgotten waterway which wound its way through the picturesque villages and pleasant countryside of the Midford, Cam and Wellow valleys just a few miles south of Bath. The book principally concentrates on what was referred to by the owners of the Coal Canal as its Dunkerton Line (sometimes called the Northern Branch or Main Line) and generally covers the last few years of the canal's active life towards the end of the 19th century, through to its disuse and abandonment in the early part of the 20th century. Also included are some later photographs illustrating what happened to sections of the canal following its closure, and to show structures on the canal for which no early views are known.

Roger Halse & Simon Castens
April 2000

PARTICULARS

THE VALUABLE

FREEHOLD PROPERTY

KNOWN AS

The Somersetshire Coal Canal

(An important adjunct to the Kennet and Avon Navigation)

Extending from Paulton Basin through the parishes of **Timsbury, Camerton, Dunkerton, Combe Hay, Southstoke,** and **Monkton Combe** to Dundas, where it joins the Kennet and Avon Canal, which communicates with Bristol and the West of England on the one hand, and with the River Kennet on the other, which, joining the Thames at Reading, affords direct navigation to London. Some short distances are raised on embankments, but the Canal is principally on the level. It is in length about

10 miles   4 furlongs   3 chains,

And is in direct communication with the four coal pits known as the Old and New Pits at Camerton, and the Upper and Lower Conygre Pits at Timsbury. The two former are situated on the banks of the Canal, and the Conygre pits are connected by tramways, for which the Canal Company pay an annual rent of £6.

The property belonging to the Canal includes

NINE CAPITAL STONE-BUILT COTTAGES

With Gardens; **Pumping Station,** with two engines, reputed to be of about 76 and 60 horse-power respectively; **Toll House,** with machine for weighing the boats; Locks, Wharves, &c.

RANGE OF STONE-BUILT WORKSHOPS,

Situate at Combe Hay, comprising, **Blacksmith's Shop with Forge, Carpenter's Shop, and Small Office, Covered Saw Pit.** The whole, including the Canal itself, and the surplus

Pasture and Garden Ground,

Is estimated to cover an area of about

101a. 2r. 37p.

The actual rents received from the Cottages and Surplus Lands amount to about **£75 per annum,** but several of the cottages are let at nominal rents to workmen in the employ of the Canal Company, and irrespective of tolls on the tonnage of goods passing down the Canal,

THE COTTAGES AND SURPLUS LANDS

Are estimated to produce a rent of about

£120 per Annum.

The banks of the Canal are in places well wooded, and the whole of the valuable timber growing on the property will be included in the sale.

There is a rent charge of £14 payable to the Rev. G. Baker on part of the land in the parish of Southstoke, and the Company hold on lease for 21 years from January 1st, 1890 (determinable by them only, at the tenth or fourteenth year), a piece of water which flows into the Canal, and for which they pay an annual rent of £10, and they also rent at 6s. a year a small piece of land at Combe Hay.

The Land Tax amounts to about £2 6s. per annum, and the tithe Rent charge paid in 1893 amounted to about £22.

Of the Canal itself and the properties in use with it,

Possession will be given on Completion of the Purchase.

The Cottages and Surplus Lands are let on yearly tenancies which expire on March 25th of each year. The property will be sold subject to all rights of way or other easements affecting the same. The quantity is taken from the Ordnance Survey; it is believed to be correct, and shall be so accepted by both vendors and purchaser.

The key plan is merely for the purpose of showing the position of the property; it is believed to be correct, but its accuracy is not guaranteed. Detailed plans of the property, prepared by Mr. Spackman, of Bath, may be seen at the offices of the Auctioneers, but these plans are not to form part of the contract.

Introduction

Beginnings

On 31st December 1792, the owners of the coalmines of North Somerset met at the Old Down Inn, Emborough, to consider the construction of a new canal from their collieries to the city of Bath. The objective of this new enterprise, which came to be known as the Somersetshire Coal Canal, was to reduce the cost of transporting Somerset coal to that city, which was then its main market.

The impetus for this development was an Act of Parliament, passed in the same year, authorising construction of the Monmouthshire Canal in South Wales. The completion of this canal would bring coal from South Wales across the Severn and up the river Avon to Bath so easily and cheaply that it would there undercut the price of the local product. Before the canal, Somerset coal had been brought to the city by pack horse and mule, making their laborious way through the hills south of Bath on badly maintained roads, carrying relatively small amounts on crude 'crucks' across their backs. Following this initial meeting a management committee was set up and in 1794 the Somersetshire Coal Canal achieved its first Act of Parliament, "for making and maintaining a navigable Canal, with certain Railways and Stone Roads, from several Collieries in the county of Somerset, to communicate with the intended Kennet and Avon canal, in the parish of Bradford, in the county of Wilts".

The line and level of the canal was determined by the famous engineer, John Rennie, who was chosen by the committee as he was already working in the area on the Kennet and Avon Canal. In 1793 Rennie appointed William Smith to take levels for the canal, and two years later Smith was appointed as surveyor to the canal.

During his period of work on the canal Smith devised his principles of dating and sequencing rock formations by their fossil remains. These were the principles upon which the science of geology was subsequently established, earning Smith the title of "Father of English Geology". He first proposed his famous *General map of Strata found in England and Wales* in 1801, from his house at Tucking Mill, alongside the Coal Canal.

Starting from a junction with the Kennet and Avon Canal at Dundas Aqueduct, the new canal consisted of a level 'main line' as far as Midford, from where it split into two routes, a northern line to Paulton via Dunkerton and a southern one to Radstock. Each route required a rise in level of 135 feet from Midford, with the Dunkerton line having the additional expense of a $^3/_4$-mile tunnel at Combe Hay. Rennie subsequently decided that the canal should be carried to a higher level, to avoid the long tunnel at Combe Hay, and it was on this route, approved by a second Act of Parliament in March 1795, that construction commenced in the same year.

The committee unfortunately decided to try a novel means of raising the level of the canal – Robert Weldon's patented 'Caisson Lock'. Despite a successful construction and trial in 1799, the masonry failed and the idea was subsequently abandoned. The committee, still fighting shy of conventional locks and by now running short of money, next decided to build an inclined plane to connect the upper and lower levels of the Dunkerton line. This operated successfully, but proved inconvenient to users of the canal, not least because the Coal Canal levied an extra toll to canal users for its passage! In 1802 the committee finally faced the inevitable, and a third Act of Parliament was obtained that April to raise additional finance and powers to construct conventional locks. These were finished in 1805, and the Dunkerton line was finally complete, 11 years after the initial Act of Parliament.

The Radstock line was never connected by locks to the main line at Midford; instead a short tramway was constructed to link the two canals, again causing inconvenience to users. For this reason, and also because it suffered from water shortages, the whole canal to Radstock was rebuilt as a tramway in 1815. Laid along the former canal's towpath, the tramway was single-line with passing places every 600 yards, and was originally laid using cast-iron plates on stone block sleepers, but was subsequently re-laid using wrought-iron plates.

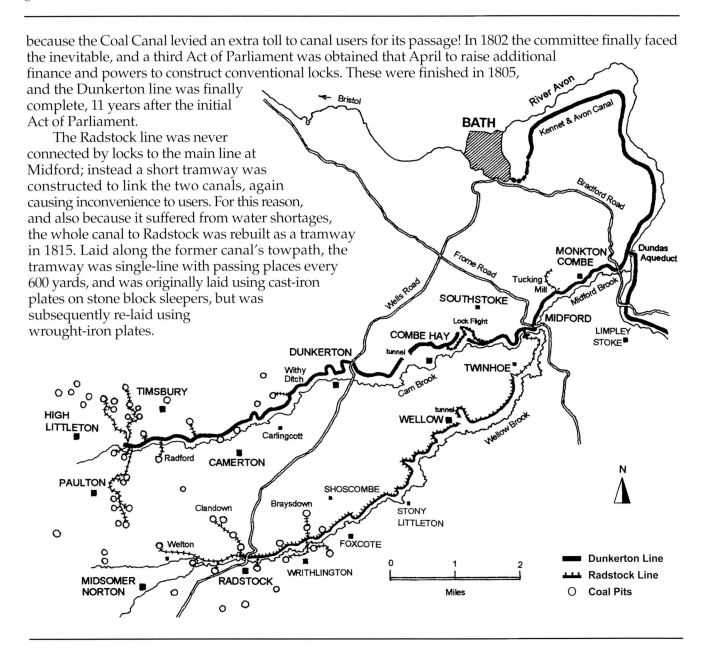

Completion

Despite the trials and tribulations of its construction, the Somersetshire Coal Canal was connected to a large number of collieries along its routes, and quickly established itself as one of the most prosperous undertakings of its time. It was described as follows in 1831 by Joseph Priestley:

This canal is of great importance in the export of coal, with which the neighbourhoods of Paulton and Radstock abound. That useful article is thus forwarded eastward to the Kennet and Avon and Wilts and Berks Canals, by which it is supplied to places on their lines, and also to others on the borders of the River Thames; besides entirely supplying the City of Bath and the neighbourhood of Bristol.

This description is interesting as it shows how Somerset coal had established new markets in Wiltshire and Oxfordshire following canal development. Trade on the canal reached a peak of 166,000 tons in 1858, but declined thereafter owing to increased competition from railways in the area.

Decline and Closure

The first railway to affect the canal was the Bristol and North Somerset's Frome to Radstock line, completed in 1854. This took traffic away from the Radstock tramway, and in 1874 the tramway finally closed with the opening of the Somerset and Dorset Railway's extension to Bath, built along its route between Radstock and Midford. The Coal Canal's fate was finally sealed in 1882 when another branch line was constructed from Hallatrow to Camerton, running immediately alongside the canal for the last one and a half miles of its route.

The canal had begun to make a loss from 1890, and the company went into voluntary liquidation in 1893. In 1894 the canal was put up for auction by Messrs. Debenham, Tewson, Farmer and Bridgewater, and despite the auctioneer being "informed that indications were not wanting that prosperity was about to return to the canal", the highest bid was only £3,900 and the property was withdrawn from sale.

Meanwhile back in Somerset, economies meant that maintenance had suffered, and the canal gradually silted up, whilst creditors continued to press for payment of outstanding accounts. The last commercial traffic was reputedly carried in August of 1898, and shortly afterwards the pumping engines at Dunkerton ceased working and the canal was officially closed from 11th November 1898.

The canal then remained in a state of limbo whilst a purchaser or purchasers were sought, and it was finally abandoned in 1904 when the Great Western Railway bought the whole undertaking in order to build its Limpley Stoke to Camerton branch line, opened in 1910. This railway itself closed in 1951, as Camerton colliery had ceased production in the previous year, but was the memorable location in 1952 for the Ealing Studios comedy, *The Titfield Thunderbolt*.

Somerset Coal Wharf, Bath, c.1855

The main destination for coal brought from the north Somerset coalfield via the Somersetshire Coal and Kennet & Avon canals was Frederick Spencer's coal wharf at Sydney Buildings. Sited near the top lock (No.13) of the Widcombe flight of locks, this was also the base for the Somersetshire Coal Canal Company (previous bases being at both Darlington and Sydney wharves), and Frederick Spencer acted as their agent. Spencer traded from 1848 to 1869 during which time the amount of coal carried by boat into Bath gradually declined. Other coal merchants continued to trade from the wharf until the end of the century when the Coal Canal closed. The photograph of the coal wharf was taken between 1853 and 1857 by Revd. Francis Lockey using an early photographic technique known as the calotype and wax paper process and this print is taken from the original paper negative. (*Trustees of the Bath Royal Literary & Scientific Institution*)

The Aqueduct, Dundas – Junction with the Somersetshire Coal Canal, c.1900
The Kennet & Avon Canal (K&A) was built to provide a direct inland waterway linking Bristol and London, thus avoiding the long sea voyage via the English Channel. Authorised by Act of Parliament on 17th April 1794 (on the same date as the Somersetshire Coal Canal Act) the K&A was built to connect the already navigable River Kennet at Newbury with the River Avon Navigation at Bath, and was 57 miles long with 79 broad (14ft-wide) locks, capable of taking boats of up to 50 tons. At Limpley Stoke, near Bath, the K&A crossed the River Avon by means of the Dundas Aqueduct, designed by John Rennie and named after Charles Dundas, MP and Chairman of the Kennet & Avon Canal Company. The entrance to the Somersetshire Coal Canal (SCC) can just be seen in the foreground to the right, under the accommodation bridge carrying the towpath for the K&A, and past the SCC's lock-keeper's cottage. Two horse-drawn fully-laden barges can be seen about to cross the aqueduct on their way eastwards, with a bargee attempting to use a pole to move the boat away from the canal bank. On the far side of the aqueduct an empty boat can be seen moored next to what was once the wharf serving the Conkwell stone quarries. (*Roger Halse collection*)

The Canal, Dundas, c.1900

The entrance to the SCC via the narrow lock, with single lock gate, is under the bridge carrying the K&A's towpath, the 'low arch' style of bridge being typical of those built along the SCC. The SCC, and Wilts & Berks (W&B) and North Wilts (NW) canals (which eventually became the destination for large quantities of Somerset coal), were all built to accommodate the standard narrow boat of approximately 69ft. in length by 4ft. deep by 6ft. 11in. beam, with a capacity of 35 tons. On the right can be seen the K&A's Dundas wharf, complete with warehouse and cast-iron crane, where boats exiting the SCC would be 'gauged' in order for the tolls for goods carried to be calculated. In the background, to the right of the bridge, can be seen the lock-keeper's cottage with smoke rising from the chimney. The bridge was demolished and the entrance to the SCC blocked shortly after the canal was abandoned and sold to the Great Western Railway in 1904. Dundas Aqueduct is out-of-sight to the left. (*Paul De'Ath collection*)

SCC Lock, Dundas, c.1983
Excavations of the in-filled entrance lock (used for many years as a rose bed) before the restoration of a short section of the SCC for use as private boat moorings. The junction with the K&A was via a 'stop-lock' which had a rise/fall of only 7 inches, designed so that the SCC would supply the K&A with water, not vice versa. The side walls of the lock, with recesses for the single lock gate, and stop gates designed to shut in case of a breach in the canal, can be seen along with the invert at the base. This unusually slopes to the left (whereas it would normally slope towards the middle) indicating that the lock was originally built 'broad', that is 14ft. wide, and later 'narrowed' to the standard 7ft. width (as on the W&B and NW canals) by moving the left-hand lock wall inwards. The former lock-keeper's cottage can just be seen on the right. (*Tim Wheeldon collection*)

SCC Lock, Dundas, c.1900
The lock's balance beam and gearing of the ground paddle can be seen, along with a running board and hand rail provided to let the lock-keeper go safely from one side to the other. The people are not the lock-keeper and his wife, but Mr. & Mrs. Welch who bought the cottage in 1898 when the canal's liquidator sold nearly all of the canal-side properties in order to raise the funds required to keep the Coal Canal Company in business. The nearby Dundas Aqueduct was popular with 'day-trippers' from Bath and the cottage was later converted into a busy tea room. (*Tim Wheeldon collection*)

Viaduct Inn and Canal Bridge at Brassknocker Hill, c.1900

The *Viaduct Inn*, (named after the nearby road viaduct which crossed over the Midford valley and brook just out-of-sight to the left), with the first major road bridge over the SCC below. Brassknocker Hill, to the right above the Viaduct Inn, was originally the main road to Bath from Limpley Stoke and Winsley before the building of the Bath to Warminster Turnpike Road (now the A36) in the 1830s. When the turnpike road was constructed, the original 1800s bridge over the canal was widened to become, effectively, a short tunnel. It remains intact and is now used as a dry dock and boat repair workshop. The field in the foreground is now the site of the Coal Canal Visitor Centre. The road to the left from Winsley was cut through by the building of the Great Western Railway's Camerton to Limpley Stoke Branch (C&LSR) in 1905, and the junction with the main road replaced by a new one just a few yards nearer to the road viaduct to the south. (*The Hall collection*)

Canal Bridge, c.1885

An earlier view of the canal bridge under the Bath to Warminster Road looking eastwards. The canal is in a very good condition with no weed growth (as is often seen in later photographs), and the towpath appears to be well used. The old road sign at the junction of the Winsley Road can just be seen above the parapet. The canal was drained in 1906 for the construction of the railway and a cutting put through its course at a lower level (very close to where the photographer would have been standing). (*Monkton Combe School collection*)

Longmead & the Canal, c.1890
A view from the canal bridge looking west towards Monkton Combe, with the playing fields and pavilion (known as 'Longmead') of Monkton Combe School to the left. This section of canal was obliterated by the construction of the railway. The towpath looks less used and weed growth is beginning to encroach into the canal. (*Monkton Combe School collection*)

Monkton Combe, c.1900
Looking down over the village of Monkton Combe with the Warminster Road viaduct in the background. The SCC can be seen following the contour of the hillside below the *Viaduct Inn* to the left, past the Longmead playing fields on the right, and on towards the village. Many of the buildings shown are now part of the greatly expanded Monkton Combe School. (*John New collection*)

Footbridge, Monkton Combe, c.1900

At Monkton Combe, $1/2$ mile from Dundas, the canal cut through a public footpath between the village and the playing fields and the Coal Canal Company had to provide a bridge. This was not to be a cheap wooden lift or draw bridge, (although it is thought that a wooden one was originally constructed when the canal was first opened), but a purpose-built cast-iron structure on ashlar stone supports. On both sides of the bridge were plaques with the inscription 'Cast at Paulton 1811'. It is probable that this bridge was manufactured by William Evans and Company who were regular suppliers of iron work to the Canal Company via their foundry near the canal at Paulton Basin. (*John New collection*)

Footbridge, Monkton Combe, c.1930
The new railway was to follow closely the route of the former canal through Monkton Combe and like the Canal Company before them the GWR had to provide a footbridge between the village and the playing fields. Here the contractors decided not to build a new footbridge but to re-use the former canal one! In order to accommodate the height of the locomotive and carriage stock, the stone supports were replaced with blue engineering brick pillars, the cast-iron bridge put back in place, and two flights of steps added for pedestrian access. Although this Edwardian view does not show the actual railway line it does, however, give a fine view of early 20th-century recycling! (*Bob Hallam Collection*)

Footbridge, Monkton Combe, 1960
In 1951 the railway itself closed. The bridge survived until 1960 when it was demolished and the fine cast-iron structure cut up for scrap. All that remains today is part of one of the two plaques 'Paulton 1811' (on display in the Coal Canal Visitor Centre). The old railway line is now a private road running through the grounds of the school towards the former Monkton Combe Mill. The public footpath is still in place and a fine section of the former canal cut can still be traced to the right of the former railway line/ present-day road. (*Monkton Combe School collection*)

Mill Lane Bridge, Monkton Combe, c.1900

At Monkton Combe was the first of the minor road bridges over the canal, leading from the village to a mill in the valley below. Sited next to the Midford Brook the mill was thought to have originally been built as a corn mill, and was later converted for use as a 'Flock' or 'Puff' mill (Flock or Puff being chewed up wool used as stuffing for mattresses). When the railway came through Monkton Combe the canal was drained, infilled and became the site of Monkton Combe station and siding, (later re-named 'Titfield' for the film), with the bridge being demolished and replaced with a level crossing. The station site has now disappeared under all-weather tennis courts, but the cottage still survives although now extended. (*Paul De'Ath collection*)

Mill Lane Bridge, Monkton Combe, c.1900
A further view of Mill Lane Bridge, this time looking east towards Canal Cottages. The elaborate construction of this bridge (which was built to accommodate both horse-drawn and pedestrian traffic), using cut and faced stone blocks (possibly quarried from nearby Combe Down), can clearly been seen in this view. (*Monkton Combe School collection*)

The Canal, Midford, c.1895
A view from near Mill Lane Bridge looking towards Tucking Mill and Midford. This is a typical view of what was a very picturesque canal travelling through mainly open countryside and small villages. In the distance high up on the hillside can be seen Midford Castle, built c.1775 in the shape of the Ace of Clubs. It is said that the shape of the castle commemorates, and was paid for with the proceeds of the gambling of its owner Henry Roebuck. (*Tim Samler collection*)

Tucking Mill Bridge, c.1890
At Tucking Mill is a small footbridge linking a group of five cottages (out-of-sight below the canal to the right) and the road between Monkton Combe and Midford (out-of-sight on the left). This stone-built bridge, shown here with later brick repairs, again replaced an earlier wooden lift or draw bridge (wooden bridges being built during the early years of the canal when financial difficulties required costs to be kept to a minimum). On the left can be seen a pile of wooden 'stop-planks' used for inserting into a groove cut into the bridge supports to prevent the loss of water in the event of a breach in the canal. These 'stop-planks' were also used when the canal was drained for its annual maintenance (normally carried out over the Easter holiday period). The footpath appears to show more use than the canal towpath!
(*Tim Samler collection*)

Tucking Mill & Wharf, c.1890
This view shows the canal winding its way towards Midford past the wharf next to Tucking Mill. The mill had various uses in its life including milling corn and dressing cut stone but was latterly known as part of the Fuller's Earth Works. Fulling, using locally mined fuller's earth, was a process of cleaning and thickening freshly woven woollen fabric by pounding the earth into the wool, thus producing a heavy felted cloth. (*John Broome collection*)

Tucking Mill, near Midford, c.1905

In the background stands the house in which William Smith lived after he surveyed the line of the Coal Canal. A plaque which commemorates his residence at Tucking Mill was incorrectly placed, firstly on the former mill in 1889 and when the mill was demolished, re-erected in 1932 on the cottage to the left. It remains there today, still on the wrong building. After leaving the Canal Company's employment, a business venture – quarrying stone from Combe Down and transporting it by tramway to the wharf at Tucking Mill – failed, resulting in a spell in a debtor's prison, after which Smith left the area. The mill and works closed in the 1940s and were finally demolished in the 1970s and the area converted into a 15-million-litre water storage lake and popular spot for disabled fishermen. Both the house and cottage still survive but the canal cut has been filled with rubbish and planted with trees. (*Paul De'Ath collection*)

Midford, c.1900 and Canal Weigh-House, Midford, c.1905 & c.1910

Midford is a small hamlet situated at the junction of the Cam, Wellow and Midford Brooks, and is probably unique in having two county and three parish boundaries running through its centre. In the 1900 view (*above*) can be seen four of the arches of the viaduct for the Somerset & Dorset (S&D) Railway's Evercreech to Bath extension, opened in 1874, towering above the village on the left, with Midford station to the right. In the valley below can be seen what was once described as a 'Greek Temple', but was in fact the Coal Canal Company's Weigh-House – a machine for weighing canal boats and their cargoes up to 40 tons in weight. To the left is the former toll collector's house, with the *Hope & Anchor* pub next door. The 1905 view (*above right*) gives a fine close-up view of the Midford Weigh-House. Within the structure, supported by six stone columns, was sited the canal boat weighing machinery – a fine example of 19th-century engineering. A boat would be floated into the one-ended lock, the single gate (seen on the left) closed, and the water drained from the lock via a sluice under the canal to the nearby brook. The boat would then come to rest on a cradle suspended by means of angled rods fixed to a yoke pivoted on a cast-iron frame, supported by the pillars of the building.

The weight would then be taken by a weigh-beam pivoted to the yoke under which a pan was suspended. Weights were then added to the pan, with a 1 lb. weight equal to 1 cwt. on the cradle (a ratio of 112:1) until the system was in equilibrium, and the weight recorded. Once the weight of the boat, previously weighed and recorded when empty, was subtracted from the calculation, the weight of the cargo (coal) was known and the tolls to be paid were calculated. The lock was then re-filled with water and the boat exited the lock and continued on its journey. The weigh-house at Midford was one of only four known to have been built in England and Wales – others being built on the Glamorganshire Canal near Cardiff, the Monmouthshire Canal near Newport, and the Thames & Severn Canal at Brimscombe Port near Stroud. The Monmouthshire and Thames & Severn weighing machines have long gone but the Glamorganshire machine is now preserved at the Waterways Museum at Stoke Bruerne in Northamptonshire. The Midford Weigh-House was built in 1831 and, as far as we know was in constant use until the canal was closed in 1898. The 1910 view

(*right*) gives another look at the now disused weigh-house but with the canal drained. The cradle of the machinery can just be seen in the empty lock. In 1914 the machinery was scrapped and the stone pillars were bought by an antique dealer who cut them up and carted them away. The adjoining single-storey office was sold and later converted into a two-storey family home with the lock being converted for use as a cesspit and the canal cut filled in and used as a garden. (*Tim Samler collection, left & top, and Museum of the Great Western Railway, Swindon, bottom*)

Midford, c.1900

A view taken from above the S&D Railway station of the local village inhabitants taking advantage of a flooded and frozen field for some winter ice-skating. In the centre foreground is the back of the toll collector's house (the Weigh-House was his office) with the canal towpath just visible next to the boundary wall on the right. Also just visible is the bridge carrying the main turnpike road (now the B3110) between Bath and Warminster (via Hinton Charterhouse and Norton St. Philip) over the canal. (*Tim Samler collection*)

Midford, c.1900

A picturesque view of the canal and village at Midford. Here the canal had two towpaths, the one just visible on the left taking boats to and from the main line to the basins at Timsbury and Paulton, with the now disused towpath on the right taking boats to the canal and tramway interchange basin just west of Midford. (*Tim Samler collection*)

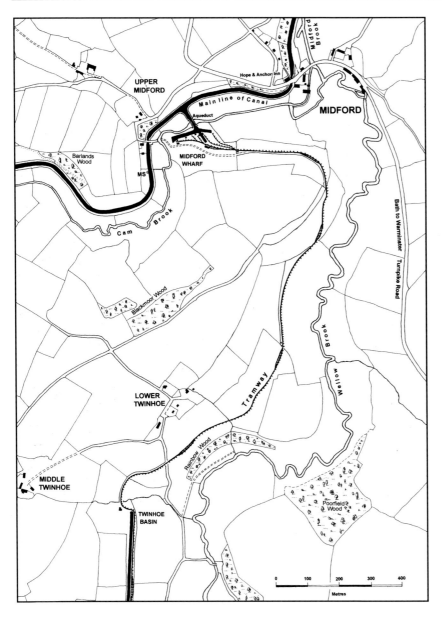

Map – Midford to Twinhoe

This map shows the junction of the Dunkerton (northern) and Radstock (southern) canal lines. Just west of Midford the Radstock canal cut south, crossing the Cam Brook via the three-arched Midford Aqueduct. Here it was to connect with the canal already cut from Radstock to a basin at Twinhoe higher up the hill. However, this canal connection, originally intended to be made by caisson locks (as at Combe Hay) but later changed to 19 conventional locks, was never completed. Instead a temporary tramway was laid from Twinhoe to a new canal basin just south of the aqueduct. In 1815 the canal cut from Twinhoe to Radstock was abandoned and replaced by a tramway built along the former canal towpath. At Radstock it joined the many tramways that already connected the coal pits to the former canal. From here horse-drawn trains transported coal to the new basin (known as Midford Coal Wharf) where the coal was loaded into waiting boats. Midford wharf was closed in 1871 when the tramway was sold to the S&D railway and in the mid-1880s the basin was filled in with household rubbish transported by boat along the canal from Bath. (*Mike Chapman/ Somersetshire Coal Canal Society*)

The Somerset & Dorset Railway & Coal Canal, 1956 One of the few views of the Radstock line of the canal near Wellow, with 2P No.40697 heading the 4.37pm down local from Bath on 12th May. The cut of the former canal, to the right of the S&D railway line, remained intact because it followed the sharp contours of the terrain, something which the railway could not do. The route of the tramway, which was laid on the former canal towpath, would have been to the left of the cut, on the downhill side of the canal, where the embankments were substantially

wider and stronger. The canal follows the line of trees on the right before being cut through by the railway near the top of the photograph. This area has long since been in-filled and it is difficult to trace the remains of the railway let alone the canal! (*Ivo Peters*)

Midford Aqueduct, c.1960

Returning to the main Dunkerton line at Midford we see the three-arched Midford Aqueduct. The aqueduct, close to the junction of the two branches, was built in 1802 to carry the canal over the Cam Brook and was part of the intended canal cut to Radstock, but became just a section of the short arm to the later canal and tramway interchange basin. The aqueduct survived relatively intact until the last century (1900s) when a combination of flood waters, tree growth and winter frosts badly affected the stonework. However this Grade II listed structure is now (2000) to be restored thanks to a Heritage Lottery Grant. (*Tony Wadley collection*)

Accommodation Bridge, Upper Midford, c.1900

The bridge was originally built to carry the former packhorse road between Midford and Twinhoe over the canal. Here the two towpaths, one coming from Midford village and the other from the interchange basin would join, one over the bridge and one under, before continuing towards Combe Hay and all points west. In the background is the former pub, the *Boatman's Arms*, a favourite haunt of the

passing boatmen and those working at the nearby basin. The pub closed in the 1920s. (*Tim Samler collection*)

Accommodation Bridge, Upper Midford, c.1960

A 1960s view of the same bridge over a now dry canal cut. Despite the close proximity of large quantities of rubbish the canal survives to this day and, due to the intact layer of puddling clay underneath the grass surface, regularly fills with water after heavy rainfall. This is the only one of the 19 accommodation bridges (carrying minor roads or farm accesses) that survives intact, most being demolished during the building of the railway. (*Tim Samler collection*)

The Canal, Southstoke, c.1900

A disused and almost dry canal bed with lock. This lock was originally one of three (there being two locks further east towards Midford) built in 1801 to link the already constructed canal cut from Dundas to Southstoke with the basin at the bottom of an inclined plane. The inclined plane being built following the abandonment of the Caisson Locks which were originally planned to link the two levels. When in 1805 an additional 19 locks were added to replace the inclined plane, the lock became part of the 22 locks known as the Combe Hay flight (although half of the locks were actually in the parish of Southstoke) and was renamed No.20. The single-storey building to the left was originally a two-storey lock-keepers cottage, but was abandoned in favour of one higher up the flight when the additional locks were completed. Very little of the lock survives and nothing remains of the building. (*Paul De'Ath collection*)

Accommodation Bridge, Southstoke, both c.1890 & Keystone, c.1960

Almost behind where the photographer would have been standing in the previous view was another accommodation bridge, built to carry the former packhorse road between Southstoke and Twinhoe. In the c.1890 view of the bridge (*right*), looking east, the canal is full, and here the towpath briefly changed sides, crossing over the bridge to the well-worn path on the left. The towpath under the bridge originally continued towards the basin at the bottom of the inclined plane but this would have been little used after the incline was replaced by the later locks. The canal cut was kept in use as

a source of water for a Boulton & Watt pumping engine installed at the top of the locks and used for pumping water back up the flight (the basin itself being supplied via a leat from the nearby Cam Brook). In the other 1890s view (*below*), looking west, can be seen the first of the additional locks (No.19 of the flight) with the canal cut to the basin branching off left. The side of the lock chamber, complete with one of the two bottom lock's gates (the other hidden by the vegetation) can be clearly seen. Both the top and bottom gates have been left

open to allow the canal to be drained (probably for its annual maintenance). The keystone of the bridge, inscribed 'Erected Anno 1801', can be seen in the close-up view. The bridge survived the building of the railway and although only suffering the loss of a few stones on the parapet, its future was not secure and it was demolished in 1960. The canal cut to the basin still survives, as does the lock, although only the coping stones are visible above the later in-filling. (*Paul De'Ath collection, top, Tim Samler collection, below left, and Terry Paget collection, insert*)

Combe Hay Lane Bridge & Lock 16, c.1892 (*above*) **and Lock 16 & Combe Hay Lane Bridge, c.1895** (*right*)
Further up the flight, the parish road between Midford and Combe Hay crossed the locks, directly next to
lock No.16. As there was no towpath under the bridge the towing horse would have had to be unhitched to
allow the boat to enter the lock, the entrance to which can just be seen through the bridge arch. The cottage
on the left was known in recent years as 'The Blue House' due to its exterior painting. In the view of the
bridge and lock from the opposite side the details of the lock's structure and fittings are clearly seen. The
single top gate is closed, as are the ground (side) paddles, but the double bottom gates (complete with
footboards) and gate paddles are open, presumably ready for the next boat working its way up through the
locks. All of the locks in the flight were 75ft. long x 7ft. 3in. wide and had a rise/fall of approximately six feet
and were designed to take the Kennet & Avon Canal Company's 'approved design' of boat which measured

69ft. in length x 4ft. deep x 6ft. 11in. beam, being wall-sided with rounded corners, and having a capacity of 35 tons. The locks on the W&B and NW canals were also designed to accommodate this 'standard' size boat. Note the low water level in the pound above the lock. When the pumping engine at Dunkerton stopped working in November 1898 (the engine from Combe Hay having been moved to Dunkerton sometime in the 1840s) the canal lost its major source of water and was deemed to be closed. However heavy winter rain kept the pounds topped-up and boats still managed to work their way through the locks until May 1899 when the canal became unnavigable. Note also the large split in the end of the balance beam on the left. Nothing now remains of either the lock or the bridge, both being removed by the building of the later railway. The only item that remains is the stone post to which the gate to the left of the lock was hinged!
(*G. W. Boyling collection, left, and Paul De'Ath collection, right*)

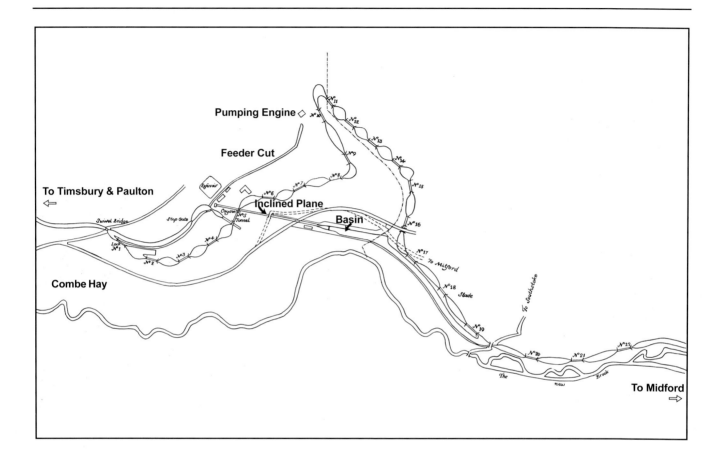

Map – Combe Hay Lock Flight, c.1804

This map shows the complexity of the various links made to connect the upper and lower levels of the canal at Combe Hay. On the left the canal cut from Timsbury & Paulton basins which originally terminated at the site of the Caisson (spelt Cayson) Lock. When the lock was abandoned a new temporary inclined plane would run down the hill to a terminus basin and the canal would continue eastwards via three locks (shown as Nos.20 to 22) towards Midford on the right. When the inclined plane was replaced by the construction of a further 19 locks (shown as Nos.1 to 19) a pumping engine and additional feeder canal cut were also built. (*Carole Haines/Somersetshire Coal Canal Society*)

The Old Canal near Southstoke, c.1905
Further up the flight, looking back towards Combe Hay Lane (note the smoke rising from the chimney of the cottage) showing disused locks Nos.14 and 15 with a very overgrown and dry pound. As in the previous photographs the top gates are closed and the bottom gates are open but by now there is no water to fill the locks. Although all the locks above No.16 still survive, none of the locks below what was known as the 'Bulls Nose' – the hairpin pound between locks Nos.10 and 11 – have either gates or paddle gearing. The locks above No.9 have to varying degrees remnants of some gates but none has any of the iron paddle gearing, this being removed sometime in the 1960s or 70s. Locks 15 to 10 are next to a public footpath and can easily be seen. (*Bert Ellis collection*)

Locks 5 & 6, Combe Hay, c.1890
This view of the pound (complete with a family of wildfowl) above lock No.5 shows how large these water storage areas had to be, required to both supply the lock with water and keep a sufficient depth to allow the navigation of boats through the flight. In the background, by the solitary tree, can be seen lock No.6, with the garden wall of *Caisson House* – the Canal Company's Engineer's residence to the left. Out of sight to the left of the pound, just up the hillside, was the Company's workshops which included both a Blacksmith's Shop (with forge) and Carpenter's Shop (with covered saw pit) where repairs to the locks (those which could not have been carried out in situ) would have been undertaken. The bridge carried a road access to the office and workshops. (*Bob Charnley collection*)

KINDLY GREETINGS

Feeder Cut, c.1900

A view of the feeder, currently known as 'Apple Tree Walk', built to link the new pumping engine at Engine Wood with the canal basin by *Caisson House*, and keep the large pound above the new lock flight supplied with water. When the original level of the canal was cut from Paulton and Timsbury to Combe Hay it was only constructed as far as the pound next to the Caisson Lock (see map) which, following the Caisson's abandonment, became the basin at the top of the inclined plane. When the pumping engine was moved to Dunkerton the feeder became obsolete and was drained and blocked by the original pound, next to the Company's workshop. From here the original canal cut continued to the pound above lock No.1, until this section itself was drained and blocked, sometime in the 1880s. Part of the feeder cut from Engine Wood is on a public footpath. (*Roger Halse collection*)

The Canal, Combe Hay, c.1872
This is one of the few photographs which shows a fully laden boat using the canal. The boat is just exiting the 65-yard long Combe Hay tunnel, built underneath the junction of the parish roads from Bath to Wellow and from Combe Hay to Dunkerton. The bulk of the cargo carried on the canal was coal, normally about 29 to 30 tons weight per boat, travelling eastwards to Dundas and then via the K&A to Bath and Bristol or via the K&A and W&B canals to various markets in Wiltshire, Berkshire and Oxfordshire. Very little trade was carried westwards towards Paulton and Timsbury, and it is thought that this would have mainly been supplies for the coal pits (gunpowder, pit props, tools, etc.). However, no details, apart from a general tonnage figure, are known. (*Natural History Museum*)

Combe Hay Tunnel, c.1908

In 1908 the new owners of the canal, the GWR, wishing to avoid extensive engineering works in building a new tunnel at Combe Hay, decided to convert the existing canal tunnel for railway use. This involved draining the canal, lowering its cut to accommodate the height of railway locomotives, underpinning the tunnel on the right-hand side and refacing the tunnel portals with blue engineering brick. In this view, taken during the early stages of the conversion work, the former canal towpath can be seen running on the left-hand side next to the wall, with the canal bed a few feet lower on the right. Next to this is the temporary contractor's railway, running in a deeper excavation towards the tunnel, which has yet to be strengthened and faced with brick. When contractors left, the site became the location of Combe Hay Halt. Since closure of the railway the deep cutting on both sides of the tunnel has been in-filled but the tunnel itself still remains. (*Freda Shellard*)

Dunkerton, c.1900
Approaching the outskirts of Dunkerton the canal was crossed by a fine stone bridge, formerly the route of the old Fosse Road between Radstock and Bath. The section of canal cut to Dunkerton Wharf, situated next to the new road (the present A367), was the first to be opened to boat traffic on 1st October 1798 and within six months two waggons per day were hauling coal from the wharf into Bath at a cost of only 2 shillings per ton, substantially less than the previous cost of horse-drawn haulage direct from the coal pits. (*Roger Halse collection*)

Dunkerton 'Little' Aqueduct, c.1955

At Dunkerton the nature of the terrain meant that the canal had to cross two valleys by means of aqueducts. The first, known as the 'Big' aqueduct, crossed the Severcombe Valley by Edelweiss Farm, and the second, known as the 'Little' aqueduct (being the smaller of the two), crossed over the lane between Tunley and Dunkerton known as 'The Hollow'. In this view of 1955, the little aqueduct can be seen with the canal cut sweeping round the hillside (alas hidden by the trees) to the right. Unfortunately this aqueduct was demolished sometime later when large stone blocks from under the arch became loose and began to fall onto the road. The big aqueduct still survives and has recently benefited from the removal of vegetation, its magnificent construction revealed once again. (*Max Crofts collection*)

Canal Pumping Engines, Dunkerton, c. 1890

A major requirement of all canals is to ensure an adequate supply of water. The SCC was fortunate in that it closely followed the route of the Cam Brook which was used as the major supply of water. The first supply from the Cam came via a leat from the brook to the terminus basin at Timsbury; the second, and most important, was made via a pumping engine sited

at Withyditch near Dunkerton, with the third being a leat feeding the basin and lower level of the canal at Combe Hay. At Dunkerton, the Canal Company had purchased the site of a former mill pond and a double-action pump (probably second-hand) to supply the canal with water from the pond. In about 1840 the Boulton & Watt pumping engine, erected at Combe Hay to back-pump water up the flight of locks, was moved and re-erected next to the existing engine at Dunkerton (the B&W engine is believed to be the one on the left) and these engines kept the 6¼-mile-long 'upper level' between Timsbury basin and Combe Hay locks supplied with water. By 1898 only one of these engines was working (which one is unknown) and when it broke, no money was available to repair it, and the canal for all commercial purposes was deemed to be closed. In 1907 the new owners of the canal, the GWR, sold the pumping house and engines to the nearby Dunkerton Collieries and the site was cleared to make way for a railway cutting. Technical data: The Boulton & Watt engine was single-acting with a 52-inch bore, 8-foot stroke, a lift of 135 feet and rated at 57.6 bhp. It had a cast-iron beam and two sets of parallel motion – one at each end for piston-rod and pit work. It was powered by two wagon-top boilers (an example can be seen in the foreground). (*Len Bampfylde collection*)

Lower Conygre Colliery, Timsbury, c.1890

One of the few photographs showing the type of tramway that linked the coal pits to the canal. Taken from the 'land sale' depot, sited next to the Timsbury to Radford road, this view shows the incline from the Lower Conygre (or Conigre) Colliery. From here it continued under the road to a wharf in the valley below, although by the time of this photograph the canal wharf was almost certainly closed as the canal was badly silted up. When a new connection was made from the coal pit to the 1882 GWR branch line from Hallatrow to Camerton (which was extended to Limpley Stoke in 1906) the incline closed, the tramway rails were removed, and the route was used as a spoil tip. The chains used for hauling coal waggons up and down the incline can clearly be seen in between the rails. Lower Conygre pit and the adjoining Upper Conygre pit were both forced to close in 1916 when drilling inadvertently breached old flooded workings and the water gushing into the mines could not be stopped.
(*M. J. Tozer collection*)

The Old Canal Path, Timsbury Wood, c.1905
This picturesque view of 'The Old Canal Path, Timsbury Wood' gives another glimpse of the very rural nature of the canal's course, through pleasant open countryside. By the time of this view the canal was in a very disused and weeded-up state. Since the opening of the nearby GWR branch line, the boundary fence for which can be seen through the trees in the field on the right, this section of the canal had seen very little traffic, boats only venturing as far west as the Camerton collieries. Although the trees have long gone this section was still recognisable as a canal until the 1990s when it was filled in. (*Roger Halse collection*)

Timsbury Basin, c.1872 (*right*)
This is one of the two basins at the terminus of the canal, the other being $^1/_4$ mile further east at Paulton. Timsbury basin was the end of the Dunkerton line (northern canal), cut for $10^1/_2$ miles from the junction with the Kennet & Avon Canal at Dundas. From here tramway lines spread out to the numerous nearby coal pits (*see map on p.6*). On the left by the Cam Brook is the batch or spoil heap for the Paulton Upper Engine and Paulton Lower Engine pits with their tramway connection crossing the brook via the bridge. On the far side of the basin can be seen the tramway line connecting with the coal pits to the north and west of Timsbury. Next to the basin can be seen, particularly in the enlargement, various coal waggons, front tippers, some empty, some full, with four empty boats awaiting their cargoes of coal. To the left of the large wharfinger's house, and just above the roof of the building in the foreground, can be seen a leat from the Cam Brook which provided the basin with water. The adjacent buildings were used as workshops, coal stores and stables. From the other basin at Paulton, tramways would connect with the pits to the south and east of Paulton village. (*Natural History Museum*)

Timsbury Basin, c.1960
Timsbury basin as it was in the 1960s, dry but still recognisable as a canal. Only the wharfinger's house remains, and this itself was not to survive for much longer. (*Terry Paget collection*)